CONTENTS

Forestry Commission

Inventory Report

NATIONAL INVENTORY OF WOODLAND AND TREES

ENGLAND

Forestry Commission, Edinburgh

ISBN 0 85538 541 3

Printed in the United Kingdom
FCIR200/PPD(ECD)/LTHPT-1500/SEP01

Enquiries regarding this report should be directed to:

Head of Woodland Surveys
Forest Research
Forestry Commission
231 Corstorphine Road
Edinburgh
EH12 7AT

Telephone: 0131 314 6122
Email: woodland.surveys@forestry.gsi.gov.uk

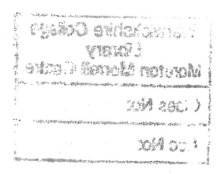

Cover printed on GF Smith Accent Smooth (270 gsm)
Text printed on Robert Horne Hello Matt (150 gsm)

ACKNOWLEDGEMENTS

The Forestry Commission is grateful to many people who helped in the completion of this survey. In particular, the Commission would like to thank owners and occupiers of the land selected for sampling.

Woodland Surveys Branch of Forest Research was responsible for carrying out the survey and analysing the data. A large number of Forestry Commission and contract staff were involved in the survey from its inception.

Preparation of the digital cartography for England was carried out by Graham Bull, Woodland Survey Officer, and Woodland GIS Officers Chris Brown, Robert Beck and Esther Whitton. Data processing and analysis were carried out by Woodland Data Officers Justin Gilbert and Shona Mackintosh.

The authors of this Report are Steve Smith (Head of Woodland Surveys) and Justin Gilbert (Woodland Data Officer) of Forest Research.

INTRODUCTION

This Report presents the results for England from the Forestry Commission National Inventory of Woodlands and Trees (NIWT).

The Inventory consists of two separate surveys:

- The Main Woodland Survey (MWS) covering woodlands of 2 hectares and over.

- The Survey of Small Woodland and Trees (SSWT) covering Small Woods, Groups of Trees, Linear Features and Individual Trees.

BACKGROUND

Since 1924 the Forestry Commission has carried out a number of national woodland surveys at intervals of between 15 and 20 years. The most recent survey was carried out between 1979 and 1982. With the statistics becoming increasingly out of date the Forestry Commission decided to undertake a new survey: the *National Inventory of Woodland and Trees*.

The survey fieldwork for Great Britain was completed in July 2000. Work began in Scotland in 1994, followed by Southern England, Wales and Northern England.

SURVEY METHODS

Main Woodland Survey

In England, Woodland Surveys derived a digital map of all woodland showing Interpreted Forest Types from 1:25 000 scale aerial photography. This provided the basis for the sampling.

The digital map gives the extent of all woodland over 2 hectares and this was updated as survey work progressed. The maps on pages 4–6 show: overall woodland cover; woodland by ownership; and woodland by Interpreted Forest Type, respectively. The total area of woodland in England was obtained from the digital map with ground sampling undertaken to evaluate a wide range of woodland information such as species, age and stocking.

From the digital map the area of each woodland was recorded and this information was used to determine the intensity at which any selected woodland would be sampled. The overall sampling scheme was as follows:

- 2.0 ha – <100 ha : every fifth wood
- 100 ha – <500 ha : two woods in five
- 500 ha and larger : all woods

1 hectare square plots were used to sample the selected woodlands on the ground. This was a change of practice from all previous Census surveys, where whole woods had been selected for survey. For each of the three bands of woodland area a different sampling grid was used with the density

of the squares being reduced as the woodlands increase in size. The overall aim was to sample 1% of the woodland in each size class.

Survey of Small Woodland and Trees

The land area of England was stratified into coastal and inland 1 km x 1 km squares and a random sample of 1 km^2 plots were then selected, representing around 1% of the land area. 1:25 000 scale aerial photos were then used to identify features in each sample square. Each 1 km^2 was then divided into 16 parts, and two of these were selected at random for field data collection. Data was collected on Small Woodlands (0.10 – <2.00 ha), Linear Features, Groups and Individual Trees.

MAIN POINTS FROM THE SURVEY RESULTS

- The total area of woodland of 0.1 hectares and over in England is 1 096 885 hectares. This represents 8.4% of the land area (Table 1).

- Broadleaved woodland is the dominant forest type representing 52.1% of all woodland. Conifer woodland represents 25.6%, Mixed woodland 12.3% and Open Space within woodlands 6.5% (Table 2).

- The main broadleaved species is oak covering 158 665 hectares or 25% of all broadleaved species. The main conifer species are pines covering 129 593 hectares or 38% of all conifer species (Table 3).

- A total of 222 694 hectares or 22% of woodland over 2 hectares is owned by or leased to the Forestry Commission, and 799 128 hectares or 78% of woodland is in Other ownerships (Table 6).

- There are 55 685 woods over 2 hectares within England with a mean wood area of 18.5 hectares (Table 7a). There are 166 776 woods from 0.1 – <2.0 hectares with a mean wood area of 0.45 hectares (Table 14).

- There are 89.22 million live trees and 1.56 million dead trees outside woodland in England (Tables 17 and 18).

- Woodland land cover increased by over 140 000 hectares from 7.3% to 8.3% of the land area between 1980 and 1998 (Table 23).

- The area of Broadleaves increased by 36% between 1980 and 1998, with the relative proportion of Broadleaves to Conifers increasing from 56% to 65% (Table 24).

INVENTORY REPORTS

In addition to this Report for England, further information is available for the English regions and counties as shown on the map opposite. Country and county reports for Wales, and country and region reports for Scotland, are also available.

Map 1   Regional and county boundaries

North East

North West

Yorkshire & the Humber

East Midlands

West Midlands

East of England

London

South East

South West

0 2 4 6 8 10 Kilometres

Map 2   Distribution of woodland over 2 hectares

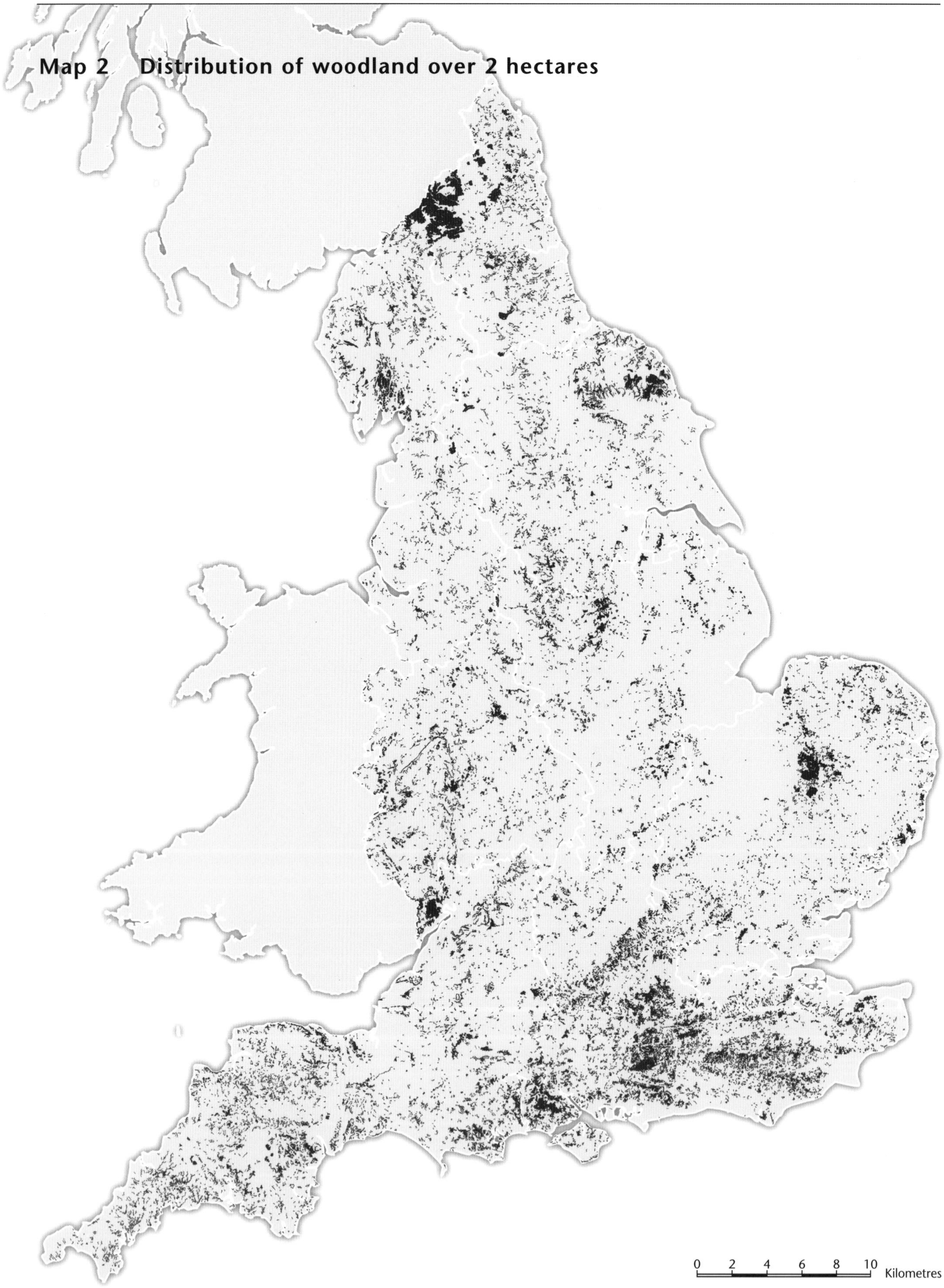

0 2 4 6 8 10 Kilometres

Based on Ordnance Survey mapping with the permission of the
Controller of Her Majesty's Stationery Office.
© Crown Copyright - Forestry Commission Licence No: GD272388

Reference Date 31 March 1998

Map 3 Distribution of woodland over 2 hectares by ownership

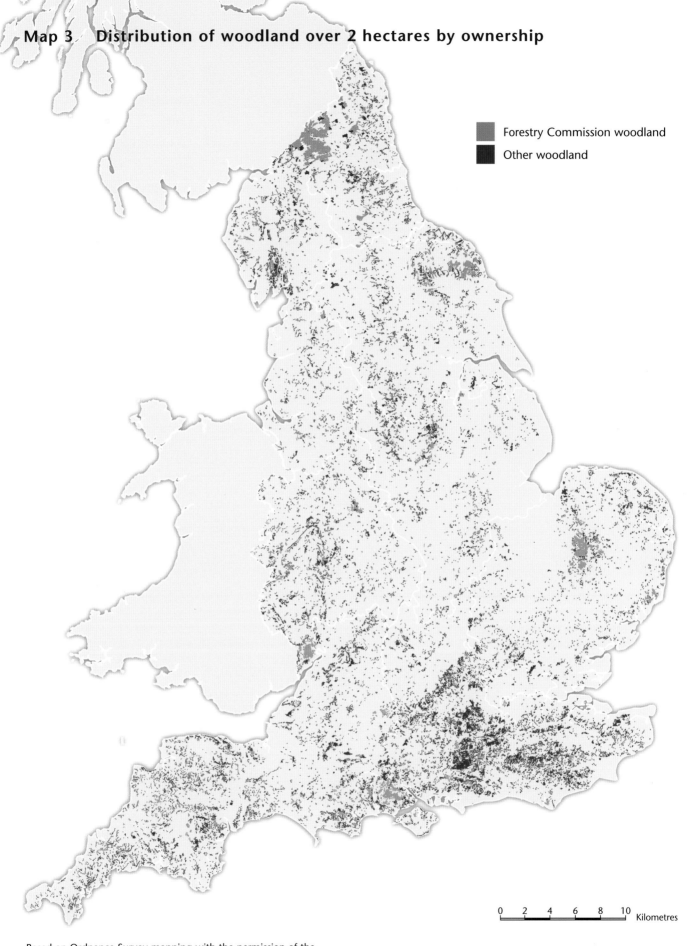

Forestry Commission woodland
Other woodland

0 2 4 6 8 10 Kilometres

Based on Ordnance Survey mapping with the permission of the
Controller of Her Majesty's Stationery Office.
© Crown Copyright - Forestry Commission Licence No: GD272388

Map 4   Distribution of woodland over 2 hectares by Interpreted Forest Type

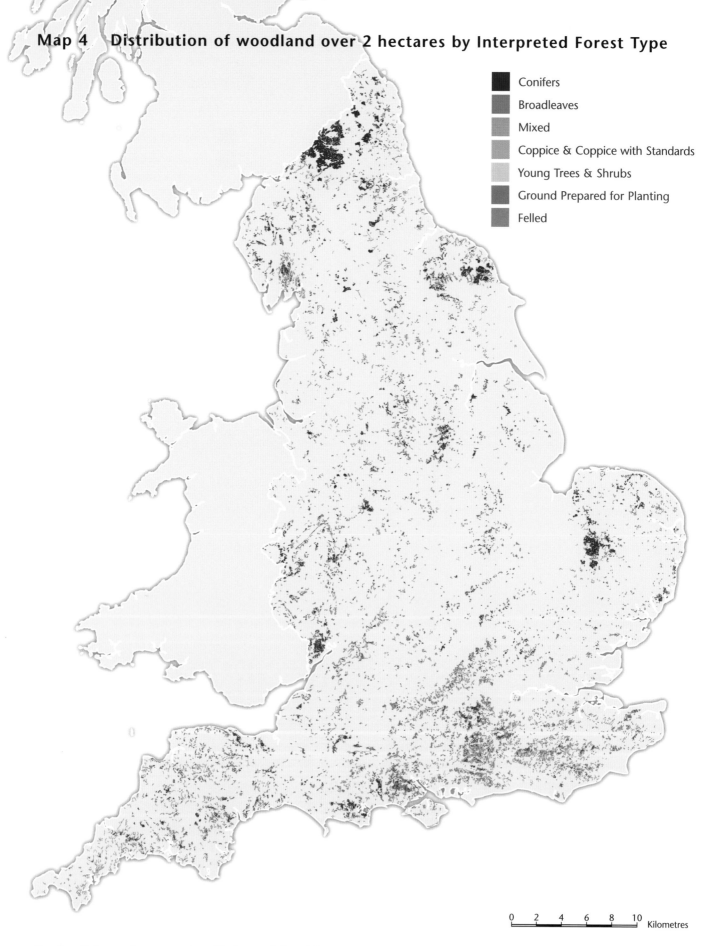

Conifers

Broadleaves

Mixed

Coppice & Coppice with Standards

Young Trees & Shrubs

Ground Prepared for Planting

Felled

0   2   4   6   8   10
Kilometres

Based on Ordnance Survey mapping with the permission of the
Controller of Her Majesty's Stationery Office.
© Crown Copyright - Forestry Commission Licence No: GD272388

Reference Date 31 March 1998

SUMMARY RESULTS FROM THE NATIONAL INVENTORY OF WOODLAND AND TREES (NIWT)

Both the Main Woodland Survey and the Survey of Small Woods and Trees contributed to the estimate of woodland area for England.

Tables 1–3 show the combined woodland area from the Main Woodland Survey and the Survey of Small Woods and Trees.

Tables 4 and 5 summarise the numbers of live trees outside woodland, and the lengths of Linear Features from the Survey of Small Woods and Trees.

Table 1:   Woodland area by woodland size class
Table 2:   Woodland area by forest type and woodland size
Table 3:   Woodland area by principal species and woodland size
Table 4:   Numbers of live trees outside woodland by feature type
Table 5:   Lengths of Linear Features

Table 1   Woodland area by woodland size class

Woodland size (ha)	Woodland area (ha)	% Woodland area
2.00 and over	1 021 822	93.2
0.25 – < 2.00	66 040	6.0
0.10 – < 0.25	9 023	0.8
Total area of woodland	1 096 885	100.0
% Woodland land cover	8.4	

1.   Area of England, including inland water, 13 043 370 ha based on digital boundaries used in the 1991 Census of Population.

2.   The recorded area of new woodland planted in England from 1 April 1998 to 31 March 2001 was approximately 17 000 ha. Assuming that woodland losses over the same period were minimal, then the total woodland area at 31 March 2001 was approximately 1 114 000 ha, giving a total land cover of 8.5%.

Table 2   Woodland area by forest type and woodland size

Forest type	Woodland size (ha)		Total area (ha)	Percentage of total area
	2.0 and over	0.1 – < 2.0		
Conifer	273 267	6 992	280 259	25.6
Broadleaved	512 768	58 283	571 051	52.1
Mixed	128 007	7 311	135 318	12.3
Coppiced	11 674	0	11 674	1.1
Copp-w-Standards	10 179	531	10 710	1.0
Windblow	1 140	0	1 140	0.1
Felled	15 100	0	15 100	1.4
Open Space	69 689	1 945	71 634	6.5
Total	1 021 822	75 063	1 096 885	100.0

1.   See Glossary for definitions of forest types.

Table 3 Woodland area by principal species and woodland size

Species/Groups	Woodland size (ha)		Total area (ha)	Percentage of total area	
	2.0 and over	0.1 – < 2.0		Category*	Species**
Pines	125 807	3 786	129 593	38.1	13.1
Sitka spruce	79 415	1 021	80 436	23.6	8.1
Larches	44 385	1 719	46 104	13.6	4.7
Other/Mixed	80 225	3 842	84 067	24.7	8.5
Total conifers	**329 832**	**10 369**	**340 201**	**100.0**	**34.4**
Oak	147 847	10 818	158 665	24.5	16.1
Beech	60 572	3 450	64 022	9.9	6.5
Sycamore	45 033	3 772	48 805	7.5	4.9
Ash	96 288	8 632	104 920	16.2	10.6
Birch	68 546	1 087	69 633	10.8	7.0
Elm	2 719	965	3 684	0.6	0.4
Other broadleaves	86 863	20 063	106 926	16.5	10.8
Mixed broadleaves	77 482	13 431	90 913	14.0	9.2
Total broadleaves	**585 349**	**62 219**	**647 568**	**100.0**	**65.6**
Total all species†	**915 182**	**72 586**	**987 768**		**100.0**

* Category   - species/group percentage of conifer or broadleaved category.
** Species   - species/group percentage of all species.

† Excludes the 109 118 ha of Coppice, Felled and Open Space areas, which were included in Table 2.

1.   The standard errors of the area estimates for the most common species or species groups are as follows:

Conifers	1%
Broadleaves	1%
Pine	2%
Oak	2%
Ash	2%

2.   Where the standard errors of these summary measures are 10% or less, the confidence intervals will be approximately symmetrical; the true value is expected to be within +/- one standard error for about 68% (or about two-thirds) of all cases, and within +/- two standard errors for about 95% of all cases. Where percentage standard errors are larger , e.g. for less common species or more variable species composition, the confidence intervals will be less symmetrical (and wider).

Table 4 Numbers of live trees outside woodland by feature type

Feature type	Total number of features	Total number of live trees	Mean number of trees per feature	Tree density (per sq km)
Groups	3 299 200	22 431 100	7	172
Narrow Linear Features	1 172 800	60 509 100	52	464
Individual Trees	6 276 800	6 276 800	1	48
Total		89 217 000		684

1.　Land area used to calculate tree density 13 043 370 ha based on digital boundaries used in 1991 Census of Population.

2.　The standard errors of the live tree number estimates for these feature types are:

Groups	6%
Narrow Linear Features	6%
Individual Trees	4%

3.　Where the standard errors of these summary measures are 10% or less, the confidence intervals will be approximately symmetrical; the true value is expected to be within +/- one standard error for about 68% (or about two-thirds) of all cases, and within +/- two standard errors for about 95% of all cases. Where percentage standard errors are larger , e.g. for less common species or more variable species composition, the confidence intervals will be less symmetrical (and wider).

4.　See Glossary for definitions of feature types.

Table 5 Lengths of Linear Features

Feature type	Total number of features	Total length of features (km)	Density of features (m per sq km)
Wide Linear Features	34 853	4 798	37
Narrow Linear Features	1 172 800	91 181	699
Total		95 979	736

1.　Land area used to calculate tree density 13 043 370 ha based on digital boundaries used in 1991 Census of Population.

2.　The standard errors of the length estimates for these feature types are:

Wide Linear Features	20%
Narrow Linear Features	5%

3.　Where the standard errors of these summary measures are 10% or less, the confidence intervals will be approximately symmetrical; the true value is expected to be within +/- one standard error for about 68% (or about two-thirds) of all cases, and within +/- two standard errors for about 95% of all cases. Where percentage standard errors are larger , e.g. for less common species or more variable species composition, the confidence intervals will be less symmetrical (and wider).

4.　See Glossary for definitions of feature types.

RESULTS FROM THE MAIN WOODLAND SURVEY (MWS)

Survey method

Woods were selected from the digital map of woodland of 2 hectares and over, then sampled using a random grid of 1 hectare sample plots. The density of the sample plots was reduced as the sampled woodlands increased in size, the general aim being to sample 1% of woodland area. The ground sampling evaluated a wide range of data such as species, age and stocking.

Table 6:	Summary of woodland areas by ownership
Chart:	Woodland area by ownership
Table 7a:	Size class distribution of woodland
Table 7b:	Size class distribution of woodland by ownership units
Table 8:	Area of woodland by forest type and ownership
Chart:	Area of woodland by forest type
Table 9a:	Area of High Forest by principal species and ownership
Graph:	Area of High Forest by principal species and ownership
Table 9b:	Area of High Forest by principal species, ownership and category
Graph:	High Forest Category 1 - Area by principal species and ownership
Graph:	High Forest Category 2 - Area by principal species and ownership
Table 10a:	High Forest Category 1 - Area by principal species and planting year class
Graph:	High Forest Category 1 - Area by planting year class
Table 10b:	High Forest Category 1 - Forestry Commission: area by principal species and planting year class
Graph:	High Forest Category 1 - Forestry Commission: areas by planting year class
Table 10c:	High Forest Category 1 - Other ownership: areas by principal species and planting year class
Graph:	High Forest Category 1 - Other ownerships: area by planting year class
Table 11:	High Forest: principal species by planting year class
Table 12:	Ownership type by area and percentage

Table 6   Summary of woodland area by ownership

Ownership	ha	% woodland
Forestry Commission	222 694	22
Other	799 128	78
Total area of woodland	**1 021 822**	**100**

1.   Woodland area from aerial photographic interpretation map updated to 31 March 1998.

2.   See Glossary for definitions of ownership types.

Woodland area by ownership

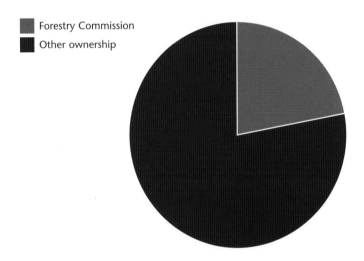

■ Forestry Commission
■ Other ownership

Table 7a Size class distribution of woodland

Size class (ha)	Number of woods	Total area (ha)	Percent of total area	Mean wood area (ha)
<10	41 351	179 662	17	4.3
10 – <20	6 892	95 837	9	13.9
20 – <50	4 498	138 309	13	30.7
50 – <100	1 629	113 121	11	69.4
<100	54 370	526 928	51	9.7
100 – <500	1 134	224 754	22	198.2
500 and >	181	278 513	27	1 538.7
All woods	55 685	1 030 195	100	18.5

Table 7b Size class distribution of woodland by ownership units

Size class (ha)	FC or Other	Number of woods	Total area (ha)	Percent of total area	Mean wood area (ha)
<10	FC	439	1 895	0	4.3
	O	43 753	185 655	18	4.2
10 – <20	FC	172	2 545	0	14.8
	O	7 081	98 530	10	13.9
20 – <50	FC	334	11 009	1	33.0
	O	4 568	140 178	14	30.7
50 – <100	FC	242	17 203	2	71.1
	O	1 593	110 579	11	69.4
<100	FC	1 187	32 652	3	27.5
	O	56 995	534 943	52	9.4
100 – <500	FC	295	61 842	6	209.6
	O	952	181 296	18	190.4
500 and >	FC	61	128 747	12	2110.6
	O	95	90 716	9	954.9
Total	FC	1 543	223 241	22	144.7
	O	58 042	806 954	78	13.9
Grand total		55 685	1 030 195	100	18.5

1. Tables 7a and 7b are based solely on the digital woodland map. The other MWS tables are derived from the field sample data.

2. The total area in Tables 7a and 7b is 8 373 hectares more than that recorded in Tables 1 and 3. This is mainly due to the field samples recording some land in other land uses not differentiated from woodland in the digital map.

3. The data available from the digital map enable the identification of woodlands according to their ownerships; Forestry Commission or Other. The entries in Table 7b cannot be added to derive Table 7a as some woods may consist of both Forestry Commission and Other ownership(s).

   For example, the Forestry Commission may own most of a large wood with some parts in Other ownership(s). In Table 7a the whole area woodland be treated as one wood and the area allocated to one size category. In Table 7b each of the ownership units would be allocated to the size category for that unit. Dividing woods by ownership can occasionally generate part-woods of less than 2 hectares.

Reference Date 31 March 1998

Table 8 Area of woodland by forest type and ownership

Forest type	Forestry Commission		Other		All ownerships	
	ha	%	ha	%	ha	%
Conifer	133 867	60.1	139 400	17.4	273 267	26.7
Broadleaved	42 644	19.1	470 124	58.8	512 768	50.2
Mixed	21 255	9.5	106 752	13.4	128 007	12.5
Coppice*	1 010	0.5	10 664	1.3	11 674	1.1
Copp-w-stds	50	0.0	10 129	1.3	10 179	1.0
Windblow	569	0.3	571	0.1	1 140	0.1
Felled	10 043	4.5	5 056	0.6	15 100	1.5
Open Space	13 255	6.0	56 434	7.1	69 689	6.8
Total	**222 694**	**100.0**	**799 128**	**100.0**	**1 021 822**	**100.0**

* England has 68 ha short rotation coppice.

Area of woodland by forest type

- Conifer
- Broadleaves
- Mixed
- Coppice
- Coppice-w-stds
- Felled
- Open Space

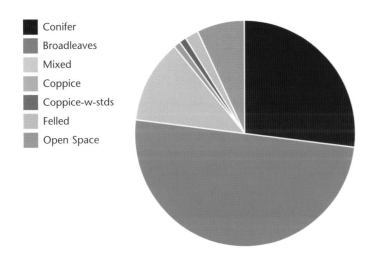

Table 9a Area of High Forest by principal species and ownership

Species	Forestry Commission			Other			All ownerships		
	area (ha)	cat* %	spp† %	area (ha)	cat* %	spp† %	area (ha)	cat* %	spp† %
Scots pine	23 897	17	12	55 225	30	8	79 122	24	9
Corsican pine	26 215	18	13	13 584	7	2	39 800	12	4
Lodgepole pine	4 752	3	2	2 133	1	0	6 885	2	1
Sitka spruce	53 420	37	27	25 995	14	4	79 415	24	9
Norway spruce	9 607	7	5	20 805	11	3	30 411	9	3
European larch	2 874	2	1	10 402	6	1	13 276	4	1
Japanese/hybrid larch	8 166	6	4	22 943	12	3	31 109	9	3
Douglas fir	8 881	6	4	15 258	8	2	24 139	7	3
Other conifers	5 248	4	3	12 609	7	2	17 856	5	2
Mixed conifers	1 170	1	1	6 649	4	1	7 819	2	1
Total conifers	**144 229**	**100**	**73**	**185 603**	**100**	**26**	**329 832**	**100**	**36**
Oak	15 358	28	8	132 489	25	18	147 847	25	16
Beech	12 826	24	6	47 747	9	7	60 572	10	7
Sycamore	1 785	3	1	43 247	8	6	45 033	8	5
Ash	4 966	9	3	91 322	17	13	96 288	16	11
Birch	9 993	18	5	58 553	11	8	68 546	12	7
Poplar	695	1	0	8 665	2	1	9 360	2	1
Sweet chestnut	1 148	2	1	9 043	2	1	10 191	2	1
Elm	48	0	0	2 671	1	0	2 719	0	0
Other broadleaves	3 258	6	2	64 054	12	9	67 312	11	7
Mixed broadleaves	4 029	7	2	73 453	14	10	77 482	13	8
Total broadleaves	**54 106**	**100**	**27**	**531 243**	**100**	**74**	**585 349**	**100**	**64**
Total – all species	**198 335**		**100**	**716 847**		**100**	**915 182**		**100**
Felled	**10 043**			**5 056**			**15 100**		
Total High Forest	**208 378**			**721 903**			**930 282**		

*cat : species percentage of Conifer or Broadleaved in the ownership category.
†spp : percentage of all species in the ownership category.

1.   In addition to the areas shown there are 69 689 hectares of other areas integral to the woodland not stocked with tree species.

2.   The standard errors of the area estimates for the most common species or species groups are as follows:

Conifers   1%
Broadleaves   1%
Scots pine   2%
Oak   1%
Ash   2%

These standard errors are for the species areas in all woodland types.

3.   Mixtures: where possible the species in mixtures have been separately recorded. Where this has not been possible they were described as 'Mixed conifers' or 'Mixed broadleaves'.

4.   Confidence Intervals: where the standard errors of these summary measures are 10% or less, the confidence intervals will be approximately symmetrical; the true value is expected to be within +/- one standard error for about 68% (or about two-thirds) of all cases, and within +/- two standard errors for about 95% of all cases. Where percentage standard errors are larger, e.g. for less common species or more variable species composition, the confidence intervals will be less symmetrical (and wider).

Area of High Forest by principal species and ownership

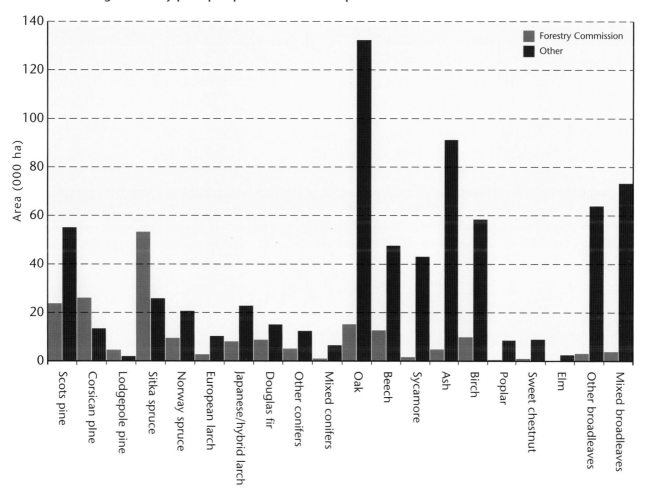

Table 9b Area of High Forest by principal species, ownership and category

Species	Forestry Commission			Other			All ownerships		
	cat. 1	cat. 2	Total HF	cat. 1	cat. 2	Total HF	cat. 1	cat. 2	Total HF
Scots pine	23 606	291	23 897	53 412	1 813	55 225	77 018	2 104	79 122
Corsican pine	26 211	4	26 215	13 449	136	13 584	39 660	140	39 800
Lodgepole pine	4 176	576	4 752	1 821	312	2 133	5 997	888	6 885
Sitka spruce	52 150	1 269	53 420	25 780	216	25 995	77 930	1 485	79 415
Norway spruce	9 375	232	9 607	20 586	218	20 805	29 961	450	30 411
European larch	2 701	174	2 874	10 158	244	10 402	12 859	418	13 276
Japanese/hybrid larch	8 056	109	8 166	22 819	125	22 943	30 875	234	31 109
Douglas fir	8 876	5	8 881	15 214	43	15 258	24 090	48	24 139
Other conifers	4 918	329	5 248	10 568	2 041	12 609	15 486	2 370	17 856
Mixed conifers	1 137	33	1 170	6 218	431	6 649	7 355	464	7 819
Total conifers	**141 207**	**3 022**	**144 229**	**180 024**	**5 579**	**185 603**	**321 231**	**8 601**	**329 832**
Oak	13 814	1 544	15 358	111 422	21 067	132 489	125 236	22 611	147 847
Beech	12 046	780	12 826	42 579	5 168	47 747	54 624	5 948	60 572
Sycamore	1 511	275	1 785	36 062	7 185	43 247	37 573	7 460	45 033
Ash	4 428	538	4 966	78 850	12 472	91 322	83 278	13 010	96 288
Birch	6 373	3 620	9 993	38 252	20 301	58 553	44 625	23 921	68 546
Poplar	644	51	695	8 085	580	8 665	8 728	631	9 360
Sweet chestnut	767	381	1 148	6 895	2 147	9 043	7 662	2 529	10 191
Elm	31	17	48	1 309	1 362	2 671	1 339	1 380	2 719
Other broadleaves	1 652	1 606	3 258	29 002	35 051	64 054	30 655	36 657	67 312
Mixed broadleaves	2 020	2 009	4 029	55 659	17 794	73 453	57 679	19 803	77 482
Total broadleaves	**43 284**	**10 822**	**54 106**	**408 116**	**123 128**	**531 243**	**451 400**	**133 949**	**585 349**
Total – all species	**184 491**	**13 844**	**198 335**	**588 140**	**128 707**	**716 847**	**772 631**	**142 551**	**915 182**

1. The standard errors of the area estimates for the most common species or species groups (in all woodland types) are as follows:

	Category 1*	Category 2*	Total High Forest
Conifers	1%	7%	1%
Broadleaves	1%	1%	1%
Scots pine	2%	11%	2%
Oak	2%	4%	1%
Ash	2%	5%	2%

*See Glossary for Category 1 and Category 2 descriptions.

2. Where the standard errors of these summary measures are 10% or less, the confidence intervals will be approximately symmetrical; the true value is expected to be within +/- one standard error for about 68% (or about two-thirds) of all cases, and within +/- two standard errors for about 95% of all cases. Where percentage standard errors are larger, e.g. for less common species or more variable species composition, the confidence intervals will be less symmetrical (and wider).

3. Where possible the species in mixtures have been separately recorded. Where this has not been possible they were described as 'Mixed conifers' or 'Mixed broadleaves'.

High Forest Category 1 - Area by principal species and ownership

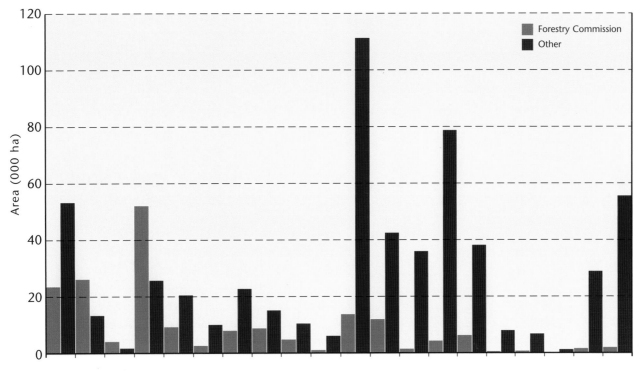

High Forest Category 2 - Area by principal species and ownership

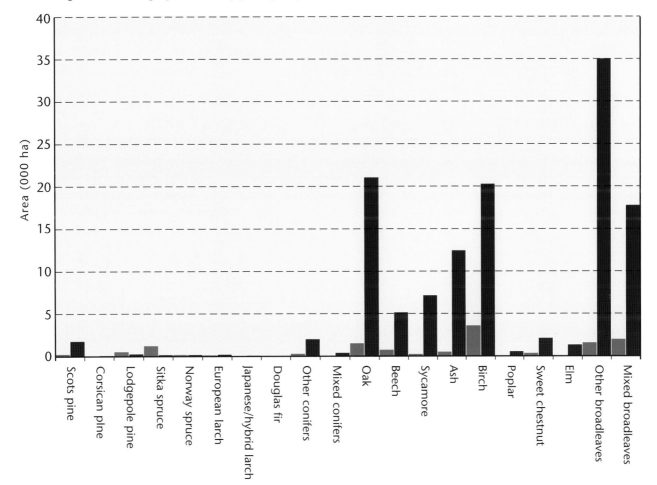

Table 10a High Forest Category 1 - area by principal species and planting year class

Species	Planting year class*												Total
	1991 -1998	1981 -1990	1971 -1980	1961 -1970	1951 -1960	1941 -1950	1931 -1940	1921 -1930	1911 -1920	1901 -1910	1861 -1900	pre - 1861	
Scots pine	3 793	4 319	10 134	15 133	17 581	11 955	5 807	3 483	2 369	1 193	1 156	93	77 018
Corsican pine	6 792	5 924	7 060	8 723	5 801	2 482	1 504	837	275	15	232	16	39 660
Lodgepole pine	37	280	2 195	2 150	1 189	146	0	0	0	0	0	0	5 997
Sitka spruce	11 756	14 786	19 935	14 341	11 121	4 606	1 225	74	24	0	63	0	77 930
Norway spruce	1 358	2 071	5 236	9 628	6 742	3 085	1 392	122	93	17	217	0	29 961
European larch	235	517	1 489	2 418	2 840	2 643	1 367	680	495	33	144	0	12 859
Japanese/hybrid larch	2 049	1 894	4 051	6 416	8 016	4 877	2 336	591	436	44	164	0	30 875
Douglas fir	1 982	2 587	3 079	6 676	5 969	1 902	954	295	246	22	353	26	24 090
Other conifers	290	1 435	2 100	4 862	3 181	1 184	512	371	583	53	576	338	15 486
Mixed conifers	488	419	860	1 406	1 164	1 557	308	390	386	28	230	120	7 355
Total conifers	**28 780**	**34 230**	**56 137**	**71 753**	**63 605**	**34 437**	**15 405**	**6 845**	**4 907**	**1 405**	**3 135**	**593**	**321 231**
Oak	5 208	2 832	2 482	3 221	7 702	8 839	7 450	12 922	16 561	8 047	36 975	12 997	125 236
Beech	785	1 014	1 968	5 685	7 689	5 613	3 925	5 707	5 252	2 136	9 961	4 889	54 624
Sycamore	701	1 626	3 373	4 166	6 380	6 376	4 854	3 994	2 151	633	3 110	208	37 573
Ash	3 125	2 932	4 303	8 292	12 631	11 653	11 002	10 913	7 054	2 324	7 848	1 200	83 278
Birch	4 322	5 295	4 832	8 130	9 208	6 807	2 935	1 687	571	139	605	95	44 625
Poplar	654	896	982	2 079	2 159	1 309	253	204	123	0	70	0	8 728
Sweet chestnut	674	575	337	677	797	1 097	942	813	402	157	879	313	7 662
Elm	98	235	316	187	185	174	60	52	16	10	6	0	1 339
Other broadleaves	1 952	1 967	3 182	3 546	6 120	5 220	2 884	1 955	1 136	427	1 647	612	30 655
Mixed broadleaves	4 069	2 137	2 179	3 228	3 040	6 710	6 048	9 146	9 758	2 686	4 967	3 710	57 679
Total broadleaves	**21 590**	**19 512**	**23 952**	**39 210**	**55 911**	**53 802**	**40 352**	**47 393**	**43 025**	**16 559**	**66 069**	**24 025**	**451 400**
Total – all species	**50 370**	**53 742**	**80 089**	**110 963**	**119 516**	**88 239**	**55 758**	**54 238**	**47 932**	**17 963**	**69 204**	**24 618**	**772 631**

*Age determined from records where these were available. Where records were not available or were clearly inaccurate age-class was assigned by reference to similar crops of known age in the locality.

Reference Date 31 March 1998

High Forest Category 1 - Area by planting year class

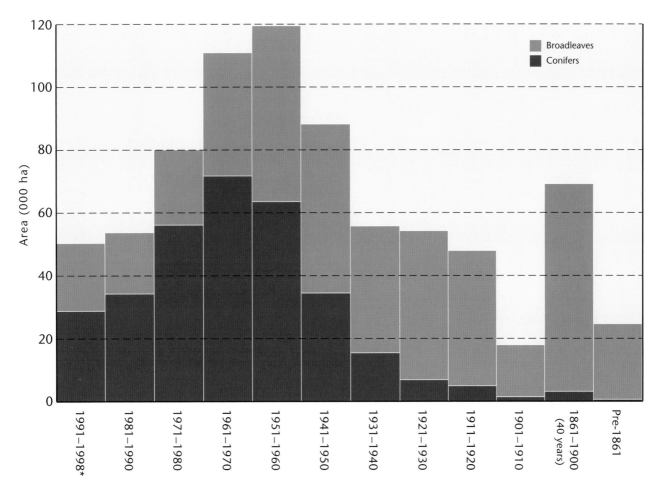

*Most of the planting year classes cover 10 years, 1991–1998 is 8 years, and the classes prior to 1901 are 40 years or more.

Table 10b   High Forest Category 1 - Forestry Commission: area by principal species and planting year class

Species	Planting year class*												Total
	1991 -1998	1981 -1990	1971 -1980	1961 -1970	1951 -1960	1941 -1950	1931 -1940	1921 -1930	1911 -1920	1901 -1910	1861 -1900	pre - 1861	
Scots pine	1 442	1 455	2 442	4 284	6 890	3 577	1 631	1 236	510	55	80	3	23 606
Corsican pine	5 626	4 728	4 540	4 857	3 594	1 312	901	560	66	6	20	0	26 211
Lodgepole pine	5	87	1 472	1 624	983	5	0	0	0	0	0	0	4 176
Sitka spruce	9 755	9 804	11 875	7 864	8 723	3 382	695	43	0	0	9	0	52 150
Norway spruce	362	216	978	2 992	2 106	1 696	872	55	18	0	81	0	9 375
European larch	10	85	189	558	544	603	240	279	156	10	27	0	2 701
Japanese/hybrid larch	798	464	622	1 411	2 607	1 478	431	204	43	0	0	0	8 056
Douglas fir	542	855	1 531	2 716	2 054	698	302	142	5	0	32	0	8 876
Other conifers	0	407	549	1 941	1 348	348	75	96	95	1	59	2	4 918
Mixed conifers	5	5	295	345	197	223	31	30	0	0	6	0	1 137
Total conifers	**18 544**	**18 106**	**24 494**	**28 591**	**29 046**	**13 321**	**5 176**	**2 646**	**893**	**71**	**315**	**5**	**141 207**
Oak	555	299	364	608	1 421	1 472	1 414	1 738	1 944	912	2 394	691	13 814
Beech	120	109	306	1 743	3 410	2 165	1 787	867	438	306	493	302	12 046
Sycamore	16	52	115	291	442	235	226	70	4	59	0	0	1 511
Ash	154	218	315	495	1 052	490	842	542	95	44	179	0	4 428
Birch	1 402	1 279	567	822	1 094	517	303	268	83	25	11	0	6 373
Poplar	148	0	14	17	184	112	49	37	63	0	22	0	644
Sweet chestnut	34	40	22	43	186	157	87	73	62	5	58	0	767
Elm	0	0	5	0	9	8	0	0	0	10	0	0	31
Other broadleaves	117	29	220	274	372	262	71	196	5	43	70	0	1 652
Mixed broadleaves	244	136	129	171	219	430	76	191	179	0	124	121	2 020
Total broadleaves	**2 789**	**2 162**	**2 053**	**4 464**	**8 390**	**5 847**	**4 855**	**3 982**	**2 872**	**1 404**	**3 351**	**1 114**	**43 284**
Total – all species	**21 332**	**20 268**	**26 547**	**33 055**	**37 436**	**19 169**	**10 032**	**6 628**	**3 765**	**1 474**	**3 665**	**1 119**	**184 491**

*Age determined from records where these were available. Where records were not available or were clearly inaccurate age-class was assigned by reference to similar crops of known age in the locality.

High Forest Category 1 - Forestry Commission: area by planting year class

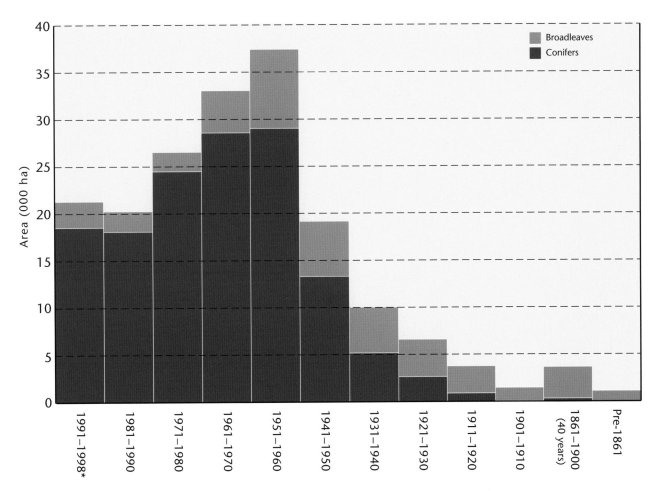

*Most of the planting year classes cover 10 years, 1991–1998 is 8 years, and the classes prior to 1901 are 40 years or more.

Table 10c   High Forest Category 1 - Other ownership: area by principal species and planting year class

Species	Planting year class*												Total
	1991 -1998	1981 -1990	1971 -1980	1961 -1970	1951 -1960	1941 -1950	1931 -1940	1921 -1930	1911 -1920	1901 -1910	1861 -1900	pre - 1861	
Scots pine	2 351	2 864	7 691	10 849	10 691	8 378	4 176	2 246	1 858	1 139	1 076	90	53 412
Corsican pine	1 167	1 195	2 520	3 866	2 207	1 169	603	277	208	9	212	16	13 449
Lodgepole pine	32	193	724	526	206	140	0	0	0	0	0	0	1 821
Sitka spruce	2 001	4 981	8 060	6 476	2 398	1 224	531	32	24	0	54	0	25 780
Norway spruce	996	1 855	4 259	6 636	4 637	1 390	520	67	75	17	136	0	20 586
European larch	225	431	1 299	1 860	2 296	2 041	1 127	401	339	23	116	0	10 158
Japanese/hybrid larch	1 252	1 432	3 427	5 005	5 409	3 399	1 906	388	393	44	164	0	22 819
Douglas fir	1 439	1 732	1 549	3 960	3 916	1 203	652	154	241	22	321	26	15 214
Other conifers	290	1 028	1 550	2 923	1 833	837	439	275	489	52	518	336	10 568
Mixed conifers	483	414	564	1 061	967	1 334	276	360	386	28	224	120	6 218
Total conifers	**10 237**	**16 124**	**31 643**	**43 162**	**34 559**	**21 116**	**10 229**	**4 199**	**4 014**	**1 334**	**2 820**	**588**	**180 024**
Oak	4 653	2 534	2 117	2 613	6 281	7 367	6 035	11 184	14 617	7 135	34 581	12 306	111 422
Beech	665	905	1 662	3 941	4 279	3 448	2 138	4 839	4 815	1 831	9 467	4 587	42 579
Sycamore	686	1 575	3 259	3 875	5 937	6 141	4 628	3 923	2 147	574	3 110	208	36 062
Ash	2 972	2 713	3 987	7 797	11 579	11 163	10 160	10 371	6 959	2 280	7 669	1 200	78 850
Birch	2 920	4 015	4 265	7 308	8 113	6 290	2 632	1 418	488	113	594	95	38 252
Poplar	506	896	969	2 062	1 976	1 196	205	167	61	0	48	0	8 085
Sweet chestnut	640	535	314	633	610	940	855	740	340	152	821	313	6 895
Elm	98	235	311	187	177	167	60	52	16	0	6	0	1 309
Other broadleaves	1 836	1 938	2 963	3 272	5 749	4 960	2 813	1 759	1 131	384	1 577	612	29 002
Mixed broadleaves	3 825	2 000	2 051	3 058	2 820	6 280	5 973	8 955	9 579	2 686	4 843	3 589	55 659
Total broadleaves	**18 801**	**17 350**	**21 899**	**34 746**	**47 522**	**47 954**	**35 497**	**43 410**	**40 153**	**15 155**	**62 718**	**22 910**	**40 8116**
Total - all species	**29 038**	**33 473**	**53 542**	**77 908**	**82 080**	**69 071**	**45 726**	**47 609**	**44 166**	**16 489**	**65 539**	**23 498**	**588 140**

*Age determined from records where these were available. Where records were not available or were clearly inaccurate age-class was assigned by reference to similar crops of known age in the locality.

Reference Date 31 March 1998

High Forest Category 1 - Other ownership: area by planting year class

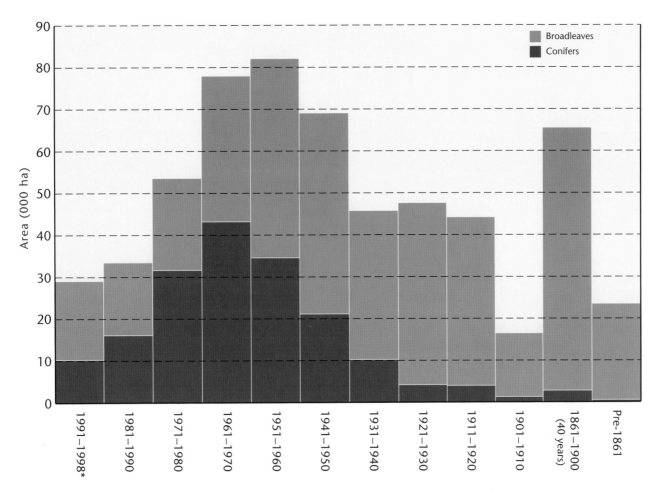

*Most of the planting year classes cover 10 years, 1991–1998 is 8 years, and the classes prior to 1901 are 40 years or more.

Table 11 High Forest: principal species by planting year class

Planting year class	First	%	Second	%	Third	%
1991–98	Sitka spruce	22	Corsican pine	13	Mixed broadleaves	10
1981–90	Sitka spruce	24	Birch	11	Corsican pine	10
1971–80	Sitka spruce	22	Scots pine	11	Corsican pine	8
1961–70	Scots pine	12	Sitka spruce	11	Birch	10
1951–60	Scots pine	13	Ash	10	Birch	10
1941–50	Ash	12	Other broadleaves	12	Scots pine	11
1931–40	Ash	18	Oak	13	Mixed broadleaves	12
1921–30	Oak	24	Ash	19	Mixed broadleaves	16
1911–20	Oak	34	Mixed broadleaves	19	Ash	14
1901–10	Oak	45	Mixed broadleaves	15	Ash	13
1861–1900	Oak	51	Beech	13	Ash	12
Pre-1861	Oak	50	Beech	21	Mixed broadleaves	4
All years	**Oak**	**16**	**Ash**	**10**	**Scots pine**	**9**

1.   Principal species as a percentage of area in the planting year class.

Ownership type by area

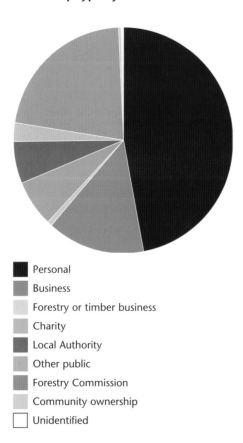

- ■ Personal
- ■ Business
- □ Forestry or timber business
- □ Charity
- ■ Local Authority
- □ Other public
- ■ Forestry Commission
- ■ Community ownership
- □ Unidentified

Table 12 Ownership type* by area and percentage

Ownership type	Area (ha)	%
Personal	480 794	47.1
Business	146 601	14.3
Forestry or timber business	7 200	0.7
Charity	68 484	6.7
Local Authority	61 098	6.0
Other public (not FC)	27 302	2.7
Forestry Commission	222 694	21.8
Community ownership or common land	3 732	0.4
Unidentified	3 917	0.4
Total	**1 021 822**	**100.0**

*This table is produced from data contributed on a voluntary basis by owners or their representatives.

RESULTS FROM THE SURVEY OF SMALL WOODLAND AND TREES (SSWT)

Survey method

The land area of England was stratified into coastal and inland 1 km x 1 km squares, a random sample of which was then selected, representing around 1% of the land area. 1:25 000 scale aerial photos were then used to identify features in each sample square. Each 1 km square was then divided into 16 parts and two of these were selected at random for field data collection. Data was collected on: Small Woodlands (0.10– <2.00 ha), Linear Features, Groups and Individual Trees.

Table 13 Summary of information from the Survey of Small Woods and Trees

Feature type	Number of features	Total	Unit
Small Woods	131 923	62 294	Area (ha)
Wide Linear Features	34 853	12 768	Area (ha)
Wide Linear Features	34 853	4 798	Length (km)
Narrow Linear Features	1 172 800	91 181	Length (km)
Narrow Linear Features	1 172 800	60 509 100	Number of live trees
Groups	3 299 200	22 431 100	Number of live trees
Individual Trees	6 276 800	6 276 800	Number of live trees

1.   See Glossary for definitions of forest type and feature type.

Table 14 Woodland area by feature type and woodland size

Feature type	Woodland size (ha) 0.1- <0.25	0.25- <2.0	Total area* (ha)	Number of features	Mean size (ha)
Small Woods	6 848	55 446	62 294	131 923	0.47
Wide Linear Features	2 175	10 594	12 768	34 853	0.37
Total	9 023	66 040	75 063	166 776	0.45

1.   The standard errors of the total area estimates for these feature types are:

Small Woods   11%
Wide Linear Features   25%

2.   See Glossary for definitions of feature types.

Table 15 Woodland area by forest type, woodland size and feature type

Forest type	Woodland size class (ha) 0.1- <0.25 SW*	WLF†	0.25- <2.0 SW	WLF	0.1- <2.0 SW	WLF	Total area (ha) SW + WLF
Conifer	704	144	5 586	558	6 290	702	6 992
Broadleaved	5 182	1 699	42 192	9 210	47 374	10 909	58 283
Mixed	862	332	5 491	626	6 353	958	7 311
Coppiced	0	0	0	0	0	0	0
Copp-w-stds	0	0	531	0	531	0	531
Windblow	0	0	0	0	0	0	0
Felled	0	0	0	0	0	0	0
Open Space	100	0	1 646	199	1 746	199	1 945
Total	6 848	2 175	55 446	10 593	62 294	12 768	75 063

*SW - Small Woods, †WLF - Wide Linear Features.

1.   See Glossary for definitions of forest type and feature type.

Table 16 Woodland area by species and feature type

Species	Feature type		Total area (ha)	Percent of total area	
	Small Wood	Wide Linear Feature		Category	Species
Pine	3 147	639	3 786	36.5	5.2
Spruce	2 859	42	2 901	28.0	4.0
Larch	1 367	352	1 719	16.6	2.4
Cypress	319	0	319	3.1	0.4
Other conifers	1 499	145	1 644	15.9	2.3
Total conifers	**9 191**	**1 178**	**10 369**	**100.0**	**14.3**
Oak	9 177	1 641	10 818	17.4	14.9
Beech	2 545	905	3 450	5.5	4.8
Sycamore	3 189	583	3 772	6.1	5.2
Ash	6 651	1 981	8 632	13.9	11.9
Birch	686	401	1 087	1.7	1.5
Poplar	1 864	195	2 059	3.3	2.8
Sweet chestnut	1 327	17	1 344	2.2	1.9
Horse chestnut	51	0	51	0.1	0.1
Alder	1 954	458	2 412	3.9	3.3
Lime	137	0	137	0.2	0.2
Elm	720	245	965	1.6	1.3
Willow	1 871	1 275	3 146	5.1	4.3
Other broadleaves	8 681	2 234	10 915	17.5	15.0
Mixed broadleaves	11 975	1 456	13 431	21.6	18.5
Total broadleaves	**50 828**	**11 391**	**62 219**	**100.0**	**85.7**
Total – all species*	**60 017**	**12 569**	**72 586**		**100.0**

*Areas above exclude the 2 476 hectares of Coppice, Felled and Open Space areas which were included in Table 15.

1. Percentages:

   Category: species percentage of conifer or broadleaved
   Species: percentage of all species

2. The standard errors of the area estimates for the most common species/groups are:

   Pine   31%
   Oak   17%
   Other broadleaves 22%
   Mixed broadleaves 22%

3. See Glossary for definitions of feature types.

Table 17 Numbers of live trees outside woodland by species and feature type (000s trees)

Species	Feature type				Total live trees	Percent of total trees	
	Boundary Trees	Middle Trees	Groups	Narrow Linear Features		Category	Species
Pine	36.9	55.5	467.8	1 080.6	1 640.8	38.2	1.8
Spruce	8.0	6.3	326.9	115.0	456.2	10.6	0.5
Larch	8.9	2.4	55.0	250.8	317.1	7.4	0.4
Cypress	28.2	7.0	204.3	1 256.5	1 496.0	34.8	1.7
Other conifers	18.7	29.7	159.1	181.5	389.0	9.0	0.4
Total conifers	**100.6**	**101.0**	**1 213.0**	**2 884.4**	**4 299.1**	**100.0**	**4.8**
Oak	1 102.6	315.4	1 536.1	3 918.7	6 872.8	8.1	7.7
Beech	103.3	42.5	395.3	1 771.1	2 312.2	2.7	2.6
Sycamore	260.0	68.8	1 264.5	2 432.0	4 025.3	4.7	4.5
Ash	1 057.7	140.5	2 636.3	5 394.6	9 229.1	10.9	10.3
Birch	98.1	106.1	890.1	1 519.2	2 613.5	3.1	2.9
Poplar	41.8	7.9	327.6	990.8	1 368.1	1.6	1.5
Sweet chestnut	8.4	8.4	14.3	49.4	80.4	0.1	0.1
Horse chestnut	59.8	35.3	84.3	252.6	432.0	0.5	0.5
Alder	63.2	38.2	479.7	2 120.5	2 701.6	3.2	3.0
Lime	58.0	14.3	72.9	199.0	344.2	0.4	0.4
Elm	92.8	9.1	1 384.9	3 488.7	4 975.5	5.9	5.6
Willow	183.3	76.6	2 205.1	4 139.2	6 604.2	7.8	7.4
Other broadleaves	1 260.1	822.8	9 926.7	31 349.0	43 358.6	51.1	48.6
Total broadleaves	**4 389.0**	**1 685.9**	**21 218.0**	**57 624.8**	**84 917.5**	**100.0**	**95.2**
Total – all species	**4 489.7**	**1 787.0**	**22 431.1**	**60 509.1**	**89 217.0**		**100.0**

1.   Percentages:

   Category: species percentage of conifer or broadleaved
   Species: percentage of all species

2.   The standard errors of the total tree number estimates for these feature types are:

   Individual Trees   4%
   Groups   6%
   Narrow Linear Features   6%

3.   See Glossary for definitions of feature types.

Table 18 Numbers of dead trees outside woodland by species and feature type (000s of trees)

Species	Feature type				Total dead trees	Percent of total trees	
	Boundary Trees	Middle Trees	Groups	Narrow Linear Features		Category	Species
Pine	0.8	3.3	11.5	32.1	47.7	82.1	3.1
Spruce	0.0	0.0	0.0	0.0	0.0	0.0	0.0
Larch	0.8	0.8	1.7	0.8	4.1	7.1	0.3
Cypress	0.0	0.0	3.4	2.3	5.7	9.8	0.4
Other conifers	0.0	0.0	0.0	0.6	0.6	1.0	0.0
Total conifers	**1.6**	**4.1**	**16.5**	**35.9**	**58.1**	**100.0**	**3.7**
Oak	15.7	8.4	21.2	24.0	69.3	4.6	4.4
Beech	0.8	0.8	3.9	4.8	10.3	0.7	0.7
Sycamore	0.0	0.8	0.0	3.0	3.8	0.3	0.2
Ash	10.3	4.2	10.4	38.5	63.4	4.2	4.1
Birch	1.6	0.0	8.1	13.3	23.0	1.5	1.5
Poplar	0.0	0.9	0.8	0.7	2.4	0.2	0.2
Sweet chestnut	0.8	0.0	0.0	0.0	0.8	0.1	0.1
Horse chestnut	0.0	0.0	0.0	0.0	0.0	0.0	0.0
Alder	1.6	0.8	8.7	19.5	30.6	2.0	2.0
Lime	5.6	0.8	0.0	0.0	6.4	0.4	0.4
Elm	37.3	2.4	204.8	791.4	1 035.9	69.0	66.4
Willow	0.0	0.0	6.3	6.8	13.1	0.9	0.8
Other broadleaves	15.9	22.4	86.2	118.4	242.9	16.2	15.6
Total broadleaves	**89.6**	**41.5**	**350.4**	**1 020.2**	**1 501.9**	**100.0**	**96.3**
Total – all species	**91.2**	**45.6**	**366.9**	**1 056.1**	**1 559.8**		**100.0**

1.   See Glossary for definitions of feature types.

Table 19 Numbers of live Individual Trees by species and height band (000s trees)

Species	Height band (m)				Total live trees
	2–5	5–15	15–20	>20	
Pine	17.0	56.3	15.1	4.0	92.4
Spruce	4.0	10.4	0.0	0.0	14.4
Larch	5.6	4.9	0.8	0.0	11.3
Cypress	19.4	15.1	0.8	0.0	35.3
Other conifers	14.5	20.1	8.9	4.9	48.4
Total conifers	**60.5**	**106.8**	**25.6**	**8.9**	**201.8**
Oak	227.9	729.8	398.2	62.3	1 418.2
Beech	55.5	47.9	32.9	9.6	145.9
Sycamore	93.1	187.5	45.8	2.4	328.8
Ash	261.5	708.4	204.3	24.0	1 198.2
Birch	87.0	108.2	8.9	0.0	204.1
Poplar	8.8	28.8	6.4	5.7	49.7
Sweet chestnut	7.2	5.5	2.4	1.6	16.7
Horse chestnut	59.8	28.8	6.4	0.0	95.0
Alder	37.6	63.8	0.0	0.0	101.4
Lime	28.8	21.4	17.3	4.7	72.2
Elm	52.3	47.3	1.6	0.8	102.0
Willow	121.9	115.4	19.3	3.3	259.9
Other broadleaves	1 562.6	498.1	16.4	5.8	2 082.9
Total broadleaves	**2 604.0**	**2 590.9**	**759.9**	**120.2**	**6 075.0**
Total – all species	**2 664.4**	**2 697.7**	**785.5**	**129.1**	**6 276.8**

Table 20 Numbers of live trees in Groups by species and height band (000s trees)

Species	Height band (m) 2–5	5–15	15–20	>20	Total live trees
Pine	76.8	284.8	90.2	15.9	467.8
Spruce	295.4	30.7	0.8	0.0	326.9
Larch	3.2	50.2	1.6	0.0	55.0
Cypress	68.4	123.2	12.7	0.0	204.3
Other conifers	39.7	89.6	19.2	10.6	159.1
Total Conifers	**483.5**	**578.5**	**124.5**	**26.5**	**1 213.0**
Oak	306.3	913.9	268.9	47.1	1 536.1
Beech	70.1	203.8	81.8	39.6	395.3
Sycamore	230.9	882.4	145.7	5.5	1 264.5
Ash	729.2	1 591.8	292.4	23.0	2 636.3
Birch	303.7	579.1	7.3	0.0	890.1
Poplar	50.1	211.2	57.7	8.8	327.6
Sweet chestnut	6.4	2.4	5.5	0.0	14.3
Horse chestnut	11.5	55.1	15.2	2.4	84.3
Alder	90.2	363.8	25.7	0.0	479.7
Lime	28.8	30.3	11.4	2.4	72.9
Elm	477.1	901.6	6.3	0.0	1 384.9
Willow	916.0	1 239.4	40.8	8.9	2 205.1
Other broadleaves	7 015.2	2 873.4	31.6	6.5	9 926.7
Total broadleaves	**10 235.5**	**9 848.2**	**990.3**	**144.2**	**21 218.0**
Total – all species	**10 719.0**	**9 848.2**	**990.3**	**144.2**	**22 431.1**

Reference Date 31 March 1998

Table 21 Numbers of live trees in Narrow Linear Features by species and height band (000s trees)

Species	Height band (m)				Total live trees
	2–5	5–15	15–20	>20	
Pine	447.3	524.7	86.8	21.9	1 080.6
Spruce	30.9	82.5	1.6	0.0	115.0
Larch	168.6	59.1	23.1	0.0	250.8
Cypress	404.6	795.9	38.3	17.8	1 256.5
Other conifers	50.4	108.8	20.2	2.1	181.5
Total conifers	**1 101.8**	**1 571.0**	**170.0**	**41.8**	**2 884.4**
Oak	764.8	2 338.7	765.0	50.1	3 918.7
Beech	309.5	1 003.9	330.2	127.6	1 771.1
Sycamore	709.4	1 432.6	281.5	8.4	2 432.0
Ash	1 066.6	3 661.1	634.4	32.5	5 394.6
Birch	546.2	923.0	50.0	0.0	1 519.2
Poplar	48.9	500.7	414.7	26.5	990.8
Sweet chestnut	8.4	25.9	15.2	0.0	49.4
Horse chestnut	40.2	111.3	101.2	0.0	252.6
Alder	237.8	1 745.8	137.0	0.0	2 120.5
Lime	90.5	65.2	28.8	14.5	199.0
Elm	1 682.8	1 764.9	40.1	1.0	3 488.7
Willow	1 049.2	2 959.3	125.8	4.9	4 139.2
Other broadleaves	22 111.3	9 117.7	113.2	6.9	31 349.0
Total broadleaves	**28 665.6**	**25 650.1**	**3 037.1**	**272.4**	**57 624.7**
Total – all species	**29 767.4**	**27 221.1**	**3 207.1**	**314.2**	**60 509.1**

Reference Date 31 March 1998

Table 22 Number of Groups by group size

Number of trees per Group*	Number of Groups (000s)
2	523
3–5	1 187
6–10	726
11–20	507
21–50	268
51–100	60
>100	14
Total	3 283

*The size of the Group is determined by the total number of trees, live plus dead.

COMPARISON OF RESULTS WITH THE 1980 CENSUS AND PREVIOUS SURVEYS

Survey method

The 1980 Census and 1998 Inventory were undertaken using very different sampling methods.

To enable comparison on a like for like basis adjustments have been made to both sets of results (see table notes). The apparent changes indicated in the following tables and charts should therefore be treated with caution, particularly where areas are small.

Table 23:   Comparison of woodland area between 1980 Census and 1998 Inventory

Table 24:   Comparison of High Forest area by species between 1980 Census and 1998 Inventory

Chart: Comparison of High Forest area by species between 1980 Census and 1998 Inventory

Table 25:   Comparison of High Forest area by planting year class between 1980 Census and 1998 Inventory

Chart: Comparison of High Forest area by planting year class between 1980 Census and 1998 Inventory

Table 26:   Comparison of numbers of live trees outside woodland between 1980 Census and 1998 Inventory

Table 27:   Comparison of density of non-woodland features between 1980 Census and 1998 Inventory

Chart: Change in woodland area through time (1870–2000)

Map Series: Woodland cover by county through time (1895–1998)

Table 23 Comparison of woodland area between 1980 Census and 1998 Inventory

Woodland size (ha)	1980 Census Woodland area		1998 Inventory Woodland area		Change (%)
	(ha)	(%)	(ha)	(%)	(%)
2.0 or more	873 518	92.2	1 021 822	93.9	17
0.25– <2.0	74 170	7.8	66 040	6.1	-11
Total	947 688		1 087 862		15
% Woodland land cover	7.3		8.3		

1. The above figures from the 1998 Inventory exclude woodland between 0.1 and <0.25 hectares, thereby matching the scope of the 1980 Census. These 1998 figures will therefore not match those in the previous sections of the report.

2. Land area used to calculate woodland cover percent (1998), 13 043 370 hectares, was based on the 1991 Census of Population digital boundaries.

3. Land area used to calculate woodland cover percent (1980), 13 043 927 hectares, (Ordnance Survey data)

Table 24 Comparison of High Forest area by species between 1980 Census and 1998 Inventory

Species	1980 Census Woodland area (ha)	1998 Inventory Woodland area (ha)	Change (%)
Scots pine	85 154	81 062	-5
Corsican pine	37 598	40 968	9
Lodgepole pine	14 258	6 885	-52
Sitka spruce	70 685	80 357	14
Norway spruce	40 672	32 030	-21
European larch	20 441	13 524	-34
Japanese/hybrid larch	33 419	32 539	-3
Douglas fir	23 434	24 139	3
Other conifers	16 308	18 664	14
Mixed conifers	21 027	8 700	-59
Total conifers	**362 996**	**338 868**	**-7**
Oak	132 695	157 494	19
Beech	54 794	63 721	16
Sycamore	35 638	48 395	36
Ash	59 249	104 202	76
Birch	61 982	69 558	12
Poplar	11 928	11 219	-6
Sweet chestnut	9 076	11 482	27
Elm	5 185	3 533	-32
Other broadleaves	52 166	81 416	56
Mixed broadleaves	47 605	88 956	87
Total broadleaves	**470 316**	**639 976**	**36**
Total – all species	**833 312**	**978 844**	**17**
Felled	**18 009**	**15 100**	**-16**
Total High Forest	**851 321**	**993 944**	**17**

1. In the 1980 Census the areas assigned to species included any associated open space such as roads and rides. In the Inventory open spaces are separately identified and the overall proportion is 6.5% (Table 2). To obtain meaningful comparisons between the two datasets the 1980 Census data have therefore been reduced by 6.5%.

2. The above figures from the 1998 Inventory exclude woodland between 0.1 and <0.25 ha, thereby matching the scope of the 1980 Census. The 1998 figures above will therefore not match those in the previous sections of the report.

Comparison of High Forest area by species between 1980 Census and 1998 Inventory

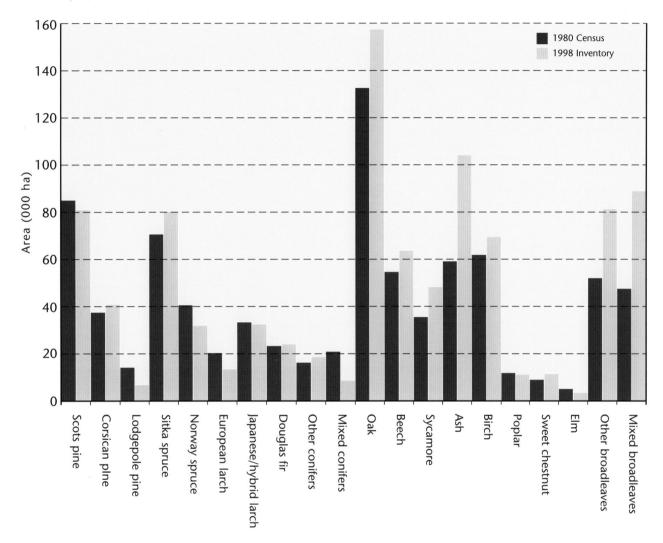

Table 25 Comparison of High Forest Category 1 area by planting year class between 1980 Census and 1998 Inventory

Planting year class	1980 Census Woodland area (ha)	1998 Inventory Woodland area (ha)	Change (%)
1991–1998	-	62 163	-*
1981–1990	-	60 922	-*
1971–1980	64 903	85 782	32
1961–1970	125 185	112 617	-10
1951–1960	141 612	123 445	-13
1941–1950	91 712	91 297	0
1931–1940	69 240	56 689	-18
1921–1930	65 063	55 863	-14
1911–1920	29 567	49 389	67
1901–1910	34 890	18 203	-48
1861–1900	93 072	72 215	-22
Pre-1861	43 737	25 472	-42
Total: all years	**758 982**	**814 057**	**7**

* These classes cover the period since the 1980 Census therefore no comparison can be made.

1. The comparison cannot be made on an 'All High Forest' basis as information in the 1980 Census for planting year classes was not reported for stands with timber potential lower than Category 1.

Comparison of High Forest Category 1 area by planting year class between 1980 Census and 1998 Inventory

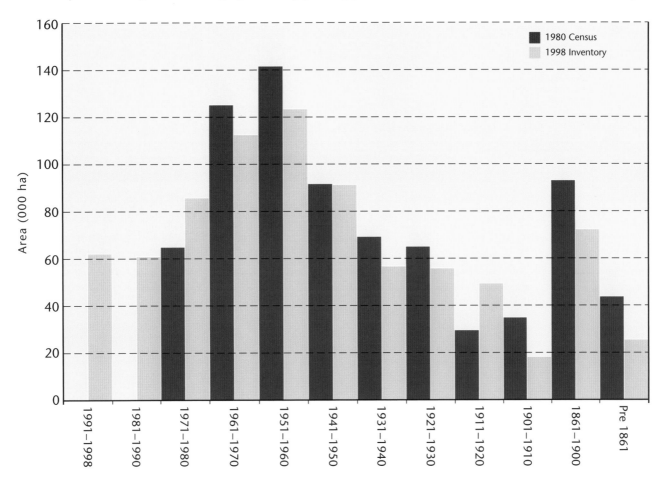

Table 26 Comparison of numbers of live trees outside woodland between 1980 Census and 1998 Inventory (000s trees)

Feature type	1980 Census	1998 Inventory	Change (%)
Boundary Tree	6 010	3 868	-34
Middle Tree	8 331	1 165	-85
Total Individual Trees	**14 341**	**5 033**	**-64**
Groups	23 461	12 998	-45
Linear Features	24 601	31 351	27
Total	62 403	49 553	-21

1.   In the 1980 Census hazel, hawthorn, blackthorn and goat willow were excluded; the 1998 Inventory figures have been adjusted accordingly. The 1998 figures above will therefore not match those in the previous sections of the report.

2.   Changes stated in this table are indicative only. Even with adjustments to the 1998 Inventory, the two surveys are not directly comparable - 1980 used 7cm diameter at breast height and 1998 used 2 m height as minimum criteria for inclusion.

3.   See Glossary for definitions of feature types.

Table 27 Comparison of density of non-woodland features between 1980 Census and 1998 Inventory

Feature type	1980 Census	1998 Inventory	Change (%)
Individual Trees (per km²)	109.9	39.9	-64
Groups (per km²)	32.1	17.8	-49
Linear Features (m per km²)	538.9	674.3	22

1.   In the 1980 Census hazel, hawthorn, blackthorn and goat willow were excluded; the 1998 Inventory figures have been adjusted accordingly. The 1998 figures above will therefore not match those in the previous sections of the report.

2.   Changes stated in this table are indicative only. Even with adjustments to the 1998 Inventory, the two surveys are not directly comparable - 1980 used 7 cm diameter at breast height and 1998 used 2 m height as minimum criteria for inclusion.

3.   See Glossary for definitions of feature types.

WOODLAND COVER

Woodland area data is available from Ministry of Agriculture surveys since 1871, and from Forestry Commission national woodland inventories since 1924. The following chart and maps show the changes in woodland area through time.

The maps use the old county structure of England, as reported on in 1895 and 1947. The data from these regions could not be re-analysed for different geographic areas. In contrast, the digital woodland map, which forms the basis of the current inventory, can be re-analysed for any geographic area.

Change in woodland cover through time (1870–2000)

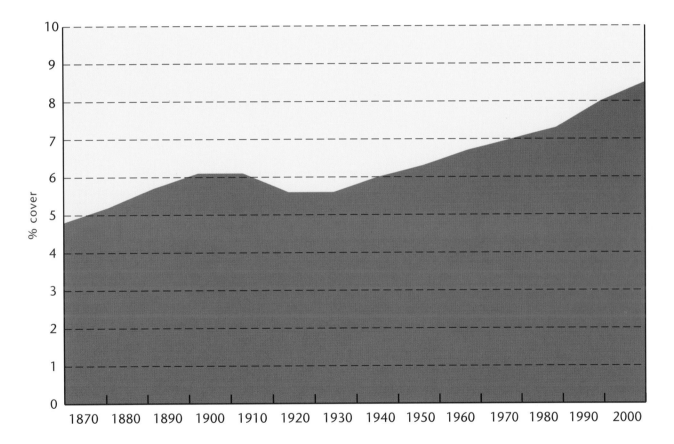

Map 5 Woodland cover by county through time (1895–1998)

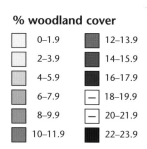

% woodland cover

0–1.9	12–13.9
2–3.9	14–15.9
4–5.9	16–17.9
6–7.9	18–19.9
8–9.9	20–21.9
10–11.9	22–23.9

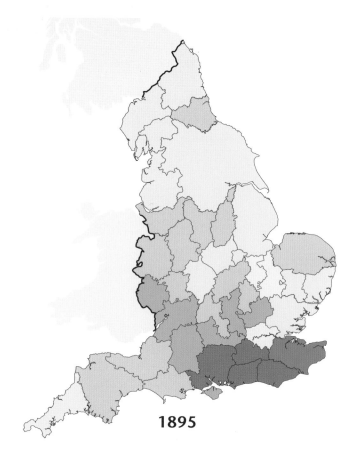

1895

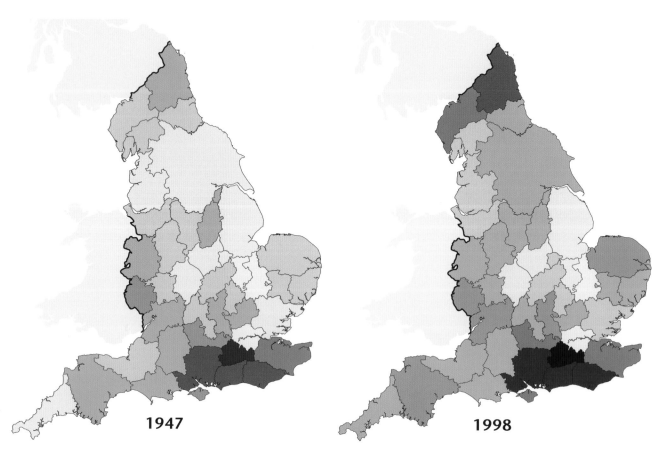

1947

1998

APPENDICES

The following tables summarise the results of the Main Woodland Survey and the Survey of Small Woods and Trees by region in England. Full reports of the results are available separately by region.

APPENDIX 1

Summary of woodland area by region and woodland size

Region*	Woodland size (ha)†		Total area (ha)	Woodland cover (%)
	2.0 or more	0.1 – <2.0		
North East	100 853	2 013	102 866	12.0
North West	91 331	4 839	96 170	6.8
Yorkshire & the Humber	90 128	1 955	92 083	6.0
East Midlands	69 709	10 162	79 871	5.1
West Midlands	84 992	13 482	98 474	7.6
East of England	113 095	26 019	1 39 114	7.3
London	5 907	296	6 203	3.9
South East	260 198	9 886	270 084	14.1
South West	205 611	6 412	212 023	8.9
England	1 021 822	75 063	1 096 885	8.4

*Area of regions used to derive woodland cover % based on digital boundaries used in 1991 Census of Population.

†Area of woodland blocks of 2.0 ha and over derived from the Main Woodland Survey. Area of woodland blocks 0.1– < 2.0 ha derived from the Survey of Small Woods and Trees.

APPENDIX 2

Summary of woodland area by region and forest type

Region*	Forest type								Total
	Conifer	Broad-leaved	Mixed	Coppice	Coppice -w-Stds	Wind-blow	Felled	Open Space	
North East	66 339	21 728	5 241	0	0	426	4 838	4 294	1 02 866
North West	35 327	42 049	9 785	82	25	347	2 078	6 477	96 170
Yorkshire/the Humber	29 138	38 217	14 403	225	268	56	1 434	8 342	92 083
East Midlands	13 693	50 106	8 779	55	112	22	536	6 568	79 871
West Midlands	21 208	60 789	9 083	598	482	0	809	5 505	98 474
East	30 699	83 564	15 414	107	1 336	0	1 043	6 951	139 114
London	15	5 357	232	53	140	20	29	357	6 203
South East	35 497	149 047	42 177	9 462	7 542	268	3 154	22 937	270 084
South West	48 345	120 194	30 205	1 093	805	0	1 180	10 201	212 023
Total	280 259	571 051	135 318	11 674	10 710	1 140	15 100	71 634	1 096 885

*Area of regions used to derive tree density per km² based on digital boundaries used in 1991 Census of Population.

1.   See Glossary for definitions of forest types.

APPENDIX 3

Summary of live trees outside woodland by region and feature type (000s trees and features)

Region*	Total number	Feature type			Total live trees	Tree density (per km²)
		Groups	Narrow Linear Feature	Individual Trees		
North East	Features	30.9	2.1	213.5		
	Live trees	140.5	37.4	213.5	391.4	46
North West	Features	533.3	107.6	1 115.4		
	Live trees	2 373.0	5 735.8	1 115.4	9 224.2	651
Yorkshire & the Humber	Features	177.6	21.6	628.7		
	Live trees	833.6	702.6	628.7	2 164.9	140
East Midlands	Features	681.2	262.8	1 300.7		
	Live trees	3 822.6	9 690.2	1 300.7	14 813.5	948
West Midlands	Features	594.8	301.6	860.9		
	Live trees	4 096.2	12 764.7	860.9	17 721.8	1363
East	Features	503.4	168.0	924.4		
	Live trees	3 885.4	8 757.4	924.4	13 567.2	710
London	Features	6.3	1.5	26.0		
	Live trees	32.4	70.6	26.0	129.0	82
South East	Features	271.3	119.0	416.6		
	Live trees	2 192.2	8 020.9	416.6	10 629.7	557
South West	Features	500.5	188.4	790.2		
	Live trees	5 055.2	14 729.5	790.2	20 574.9	863
Total	**Features**	**3 299.2**	**1 172.8**	**6 276.8**		
	Live trees	**22 431.1**	**60 509.1**	**6 276.8**	**89 217.0**	**684**

*Area of regions used to derive tree density per km² based on digital boundaries used in 1991 Census of Population.

1.   See Glossary for definitions of feature types

APPENDIX 4

Summary of number and length of Linear Features by region

Region*	Total number of features (000s)	Total length of features (km)	Density (m per km²)
North East	2	169	20
North West	110	9 960	703
Yorkshire/the Humber	24	1 748	113
East Midlands	270	17 966	1 150
West Midlands	310	23 322	1 793
East	173	14 325	749
London	2	223	141
South East	120	12 433	651
South West	197	15 833	664
Total	**1 207**	**95 979**	**736**

* Area of regions used to derive length per km² based on digital boundaries used in 1991 Census of Population.

GLOSSARY

Woodland

In the United Kingdom woodland is defined as land with a minimum area of 0.1 ha under stands of trees with, or with the potential to achieve, tree crown cover of more than 20%. Areas of open space integral to the woodland are also included. Orchards and urban woodland between 0.1 and 2 ha are excluded. Intervening land-classes such as roads, rivers or pipelines are disregarded if less than 50 m in extent. 'Scrubby' vegetation is not included as a separate category but as Conifer, Broadleaved or Mixed tree types. There is additional information on the quality of woodland within the inventory database.

Woodland of 2 ha and over, and with a minimum width of 50 m, is included in the Main Woodland Survey; other woodland and trees are assessed in the Survey of Small Woods and Trees.

Interpreted Forest Types

The woodland map derived from aerial photographs is differentiated into Interpreted Forest Types (IFTs) which are: Conifer, Broadleaved, Mixed, Coppice, Coppice-with-Standards, Shrubs, Young Trees, Ground Prepared for Planting and Felled. Note that forest types (see below) based on ground survey data are used for reporting purposes because they are more reliable.

High Forest

All woodland except stands managed as Coppice or Coppice-with-Standards with, or with the potential to achieve, a tree cover of more than 20%. Two categories of High Forest are recognised:

- **High Forest Category 1**

  Stands which are, or could become, capable of producing wood of a size and quality suitable for sawlogs.

- **High Forest Category 2**

  Stands of lower quality than High Forest Category 1.

Mixtures

Where possible the species in mixtures have been separately recorded. Where this has not been possible they were described as 'Mixed conifers' or 'Mixed broadleaves'.

Forest Types

- **Conifer**

  Woodland containing more than 80% by area of coniferous species.

- **Broadleaved**

  Woodland containing more than 80% by area of broadleaved species.

- **Mixed**

  A combination of broadleaved and coniferous species where each category occupies at least 20% of the canopy (see note on Mixtures above).

- **Coppice**

Crops of marketable broadleaved species that have at least 2 stems per stool and are either being worked or are capable of being worked on rotation. With the exception of hazel coppice more than half the stems should be capable of producing 1 m timber lengths of good form.

- **Coppice with Standards**

Two-storey stands where the overstorey consists of at least 25 stems per ha that are older than the understorey of worked coppice by at least one coppice rotation.

- **Felled**

Woodland areas that have been felled or stands where the stocking has been reduced to less than 20% and where it is expected that these areas will be replanted.

- **Windblow**

Areas of blown woodland which remain uncleared and not regenerated.

- **Open Space**

Areas within a woodland that are not covered by trees, but are integral to the woodland, such as open areas, streamsides, deer glades, rides and forest roads.

Ownership types

- **Other ownership**

Woodland other than that owned by, or leased to, the Forestry Commission:

- **Personal**

types of private occupation, e.g. individuals, private family trusts and family partnerships.

- **Private forestry or timber business**

owned by wood processing industry. This category does not include forest management companies.

- **Other private business**

occupiers, e.g. companies, partnerships, syndicates and pension funds.

- **Local Authority**

region, county, district or other council.

- **Other public bodies (not FC)**

Government department/agency, nationalised industry, etc.

- **Charitable organisations**

organisations funded by voluntary public subscription, e.g. National Trust, churches and colleges.

- **Community ownership or common land**

the common property of all members of the community.

• **Forestry Commission**

Land owned by or leased to the Forestry Commission

Feature types

• **Small Wood**

A woodland with an area of 0.1 ha or over, but less than 2 ha.

• **Group**

A group containing two or more trees with an area less than 0.1 ha.

• **Individual Tree**

A tree with a crown that has no contact with any other tree crown, and which is at least 2m tall. Two types of Individual Tree are recognised:

- Boundary Tree (an Individual Tree on a boundary)

- Middle Tree (an Individual Tree not on a boundary)

• **Linear Feature**

A feature with a length of 25 m or more, and one which is at least four times as long as it is broad. It can be up to 50 m wide or as narrow as a single line of trees. Two types of Linear Feature are recognised:

- Narrow Linear Features (with a width of 16 m or less)

- Wide Linear Features (with a width greater than 16 m)

NOTES